Cherry Picking
for the
Lazy Bums

SWAPNA GOPINATH

Envision Earth Media

First published in paperback in 2019
By Envision Earth Media
A division of The Open Circle LLC, USA

ISBN: 9781733083805
Price: US $6.49

Envision Earth Media,
A division of The Open Circle LLC,
902 Gribbin Ln 3B,
Toledo OH 43612,
USA.
www.envisionearthmedia.com

"Blissings! You 'injoy' your journey through Swapna's book, and are able to easily and effortlessly incorporate some, if not all, of the 'onederfull' suggestions shared within its pages that you too may say, I am loving, living a life of absolute 'fabyoubliss'!"

- **Rev. Rhonda Sheryl Lipstein**
  www.rhondasheryllipstein.com

"The 'Law of Attraction' is a starting point for those who wish to manifest their desires in life, and 'Who doesn't?' you might ask. Swapna does a fine job in explaining quite simply how you can meditate and use the power of your mind to attract whatever you wish for, with routine examples that you can easily relate to. An enjoyable read for beginners."

- **Swati Prakash, Spiritual Author**
  www.swatiprakash.com

CONTENTS

CONTENTS (Continued)

ABOUT THE AUTHOR

Swapna Gopinath was born in the Kerala state of India, renowned as 'God's Own Country,' and was raised in another equally beautiful place near the sea, Goa. Armed with a Masters in Business Administration and a passion for numbers, she was a part of the talent acquisition function for various multinationals for over 12 years. Currently, she is the Chief Marketing and Promotions Manager of Envision Earth Media and Envision Earth Magazine.

Swapna grew up with an ardent interest in reading. She has now ventured into writing. In her spare time, she enjoys travelling, reading and trying different cuisines worldwide. This online book, on the subject of the Law of Attraction, is her first spiritual book. Her extensive research on this topic besides the real-life miracles she has experienced helped her compile this book which presents practical and simplified methods that as many people as possible can practise to enrich their lives.

FOREWORD

Swapna Gopinath has written a unique manual for people to master the magic of manifestation. This book is different as it addresses the missing links in the popular understanding of LOA. Swapna presents a plethora of practical methods with clear explanations of the steps involved in turning our dreams into reality. She has used enlightening anecdotes and examples of her own experience to illustrate the techniques. Instead of the passivity that has often been pointed out by the critics of the LOA movement, she emphasizes the need for a proactive approach. Methods like affirmations, visualization and a positive attitude must be coupled with appropriate action to create the conditions for your goals to materialize.

I am glad about the opportunity to offer editorial support to this talented writer whose infectious enthusiasm to help people enrich their lives will surely inspire every reader. I wish Swapna a bright future as a writer.

Warm Regards,

Prabhath P.
Chief Operations Officer and Editor-in-Chief,
Envision Earth Media
www.envisionearthmedia.com

PREFACE

I have embarked on writing this book because I believe everyone should be able to live their dream life. I have been incorporating these practices in my life for the last 10 years and these methods have helped me immensely. Hence, I think it will be of great help to many people in different ways.

Although I personally practise and see a lot of people attracting whatever they want easily and effortlessly, I also wish to bring to your attention that not every technique works for everyone. What might work for one person need not work for another individual, and yet you are able to manifest anything you wish for by applying one or several of the methods, penned down in this book.

I have listed some methods in the most simplified manner so that each one of you can follow them, and discover what works for you personally. In fact, I have come across people who cannot form a single positive sentence about themselves. They either do not know how to write it down or have grammar issues, yet I would suggest that they practise any of the methods mentioned in this book for the purpose of manifesting their heart's desires.

The word 'impossible' too has a possibility within it, so give it your all as you have nothing to lose but everything to gain by adopting the methods you like and discarding the ones you don't. I am so excited for each one of you who are on your personal journey to manifest the greatest desires of your lives. Remember that anything and everything is possible provided you believe with complete faith that you can and you are capable of attracting it in your life effortlessly, as you are the creator of your life. If I can do it, if millions of people around the world can do it, so can you!

Love,
Swapna Gopinath

ACKNOWLEDGMENTS

This book is my first spiritual book and I thank the writers of several spiritual books who helped me make my life truly magnificent where I am finally doing what I always loved: Writing!

I would like to thank Mr. Prabhath P, who tirelessly put in the effort to work closely on the project without which this book would not see the light of the day. On a lighter note, it was indeed surprising to realize that the manuscript was not only being reviewed with hawk eyes but it was also subjected to a pair of the sharpest scissors that had the incredible capability to chop off large chunks, in the name of editing! But jokes apart, I am immensely grateful for the remarkable help in the editing area. I thank him for his invaluable editorial assistance and foreword. I am hoping he doesn't use his sharp scissors out here as well!!!

My special gratitude to Ms. Swati Prakash and Rev. Rhonda Sheryl Lipstein for taking time out of their extremely busy schedule to read my book and write a few lines of appreciation about it.

My special gratitude for Mr. Shibin, who creatively designed the cover page in tune with my taste.

I always wanted to write and the nudge was much needed and is welcome forever. A shout of thanks to Jijith Nallika. Thankyou my friend!

A special 'Thank you' to all my dear friends like Sushmita, Sanjeeta, Jina and Preety who were my support all through the book by proving data and insights.

My never-ending thanks to my Parents. My dad is no more, but he has been truly my inspiration throughout my life's journey. My darling mom is the pillar of my strength. She continuously encourages me to chase my dreams in every phase of my life.

I want to thank the sunshine of my life, Nihal Nadayil, who is my heartbeat in the literal sense, for his consistent inspiration and endless encouragement. He has taught me to live all my dreams. I thank God for every miracle that has happened and continues to happen in my life. I am eternally grateful for the divine guidance.

1. OBSERVE YOUR THOUGHTS

Wow! You are so damn lucky! You can think! A lot of people are not as blessed as you are. The gift of thinking brings about roughly 60,000 to 70,000 thoughts daily. So that makes it about 40 to 48 thoughts every minute per person. Thinking constitutes positive thoughts as well as negative thoughts. No matter what you think, always remember, your thoughts do have an impact on your life.

Now that you know your thoughts have an impact on your life, you need to be very alert. Start observing your thoughts. No matter how tempting it might be to say something bad about someone (gossip), or to think negatively about your life's situation (self-pity) or to feel angry or jealous about someone (stress and insecurity), don't do it. Stop right there. It is going to do you no good. So change the way you think or feel as soon as you realize the path of your thoughts.

The moment you think of anything that is negative, you can intentionally mention something positive immediately so that the negative thought is nullified.

Ensure that every time you say anything negative, you switch to ending it with a positive statement. Keep doing it until you have absolute control over every negative sentence that you tend to think.

If you are in the habit of thinking negatively for hours together about one particular person or an instance that seems to bother you, try to observe your thought pattern and cap it there itself. Are you not giving that particular person or that specific instance too much importance? Is it worth? By doing so, you are not just ruining your life and your health but you are actively turning your life toxic.

Let's go step by step to erase it. First and foremost, keep a tab of your thoughts. One option for you is to take a note pad and jot down all your negative thoughts. By doing this, in a way, you are venting it out of your system. We can start focusing on one area of your life, to begin with. If you want to highlight your current love life that's not going the way you want, and your thoughts are only making you feel worse, waste no time. You can start by writing the thing that are not going well for you or for the relationship. Keep writing until you feel that there can't be anything more to write about.

Some of you might feel like crying while writing. If you feel so, do it. If you feel like yelling or abusing while you write, do that too. Don't bottle up anything. Let it go out of your system for good. Let this be a venting out process in the bargain. You need to get this done and over with so that you can make a change in yourself intentionally.

2

After you have written down the negative instances, experiences or behavior in your current relationship, just leave it aside. Let it go for good. Take a deep breath and ignore it forever.

Start thinking good thoughts. Focus on being happy and observe your happy thoughts. You can begin writing down whatever makes you happy. Maybe, the memory of something that someone has done for you makes you happy. Perhaps, the remembrance of a vacation that you had a while ago brings you happiness. Maybe, recalling a compliment that you got at office makes you happy or something in a particular relationship is a source of happiness for you.

If you are trying to better your relationship but cannot bring yourself to note a single point of happiness, as your current relationship has deteriorated downhill, then think about what made you happy enough to pursue it in the first place? I am certain you will come up with umpteen reasons. If this too fails for whatever reasons, then you can alternatively write down one of your dream experiences that you would love to experience with your partner in the future, especially a wish that might still be a fragment of your imagination that exists only as a wonderful fantasy. Wait no more! You can now turn everything you desire into reality.

For instance, you might still be yearning to have a vacation with your partner in Spain where you would like to spend some time solely with him, explore his personality, and see a more romantic and caring side of him which you probably haven't been seeing of late.

Write down everything that you desire. Write it all down as if it is a dream that is manifesting in reality. You need to be very clear and vivid like it is occurring right in front of you. Writing down anything requires some sort of imagination. So go ahead and use yours. Does it feel like it is happening in reality? Be as natural as possible. Keep recollecting and enjoying occasions that made you happy in the past and based on those special memories, pen down similar instances that you would welcome in the future.

All along, you need to ensure that your thoughts or expressions don't come across as a desperate need. It has to be more like a happy experience than a need-based experience because you need no one to make you happy. You need no one to complete you. You do not need anything external to be happy. You depend on yourself and not others to make you happy. Every time you rely on your boyfriend, husband, or lover to make you happy, it will result in a temporary phase of happiness and cannot fill the void, on a long-term basis. Your dependency on anything external will only create unhappiness in your life.

The thoughts you think shape your life. If you keep thinking that you are not capable of earning well, over a period of time, it's exactly this thought that you will manifest. You would begin to notice that you always find yourself in financially sticky situations and you are most often powerless to bail yourself out of the situation because you lack a good income. You will find that none of your dreams come true and this thought will create a scenario that resembles a pack of cards crumbling, with nothing manifesting around you.

For example, how many of you already think that buying a fancy car or a house is out of your reach? This expectation is exactly what you have been attracting until now. Break free of this mind-set that tends to condition your thought process.

Monitor your thoughts and give no room for anything negative. Let happy and positive thoughts capture your mind as your conscious thoughts form more than 80% of your thoughts. These conscious thoughts impact your subconscious thoughts, which in turn manifest into reality.

The first step to manifestation is our thoughts… let's intentionally begin to sieve the good ones from the bad ones!

2. LOVE YOURSELF

To love your own self is the simplest thing that one can do in life. Yet, it seems impossible for many people. Frequently, I come across people who judge themselves very critically. These are the people who tend to have a list of negative attributes about themselves overweighing the positives ones that they are bestowed with.

I am sure most of you out there can resonate with what I am writing because it has become a regular phenomenon to hear comments like "I am too dark," or "I am too fat," or "I am too thin," or "Nobody likes me," or "I am so unhappy in my life while everyone else is happy," or "Why can't I be as successful as him or her?"

Well, who is stopping you from achieving whatever you want in your life? The answer is YOU.

Now that you have the answer to your question, you need to quit complaining about yourself and focus on all the good aspects of your personality or anything that's worthy in your life. Trust me! The list is rather long when it comes to sorting the good that you are blessed with. So chalk out all the positives in yourself. It can't be that difficult.

I know of a lot of people who admit that even after trying hard, they are unable to find any positive aspects in their personality. Here, I would like to remind them of several people on planet Earth who are less fortunate than them in countless ways. I personally know people who are terminally ill with one leg almost in the grave or bedridden for years; yet they love life and their amazing zeal to live their lives with a smile on their face, every single day, is infectious, leaving many around them often speechless.

If the person who is confined to the bed is not bound by his shortcomings, then what confines you to focus only on your negative attributes? Let's value the special qualities in each of us that make us, 'ME.'

You need to be able to highlight your positive attributes. There is only one special YOU in this whole world and you are irreplaceable. Solely for that reason, you need to love yourself truly. You need to love yourself deeply. You need to love yourself madly. If you feel like it's a chore to appreciate yourself daily, go in for a makeover. Change your clothes, makeup, shoes, have a trendy haircut or transform whatever it is that needs to be changed so that you are convinced enough to recognize your own worth. I would even go further and suggest that you splurge lavishly on yourself.

I am pointing this out specifically because most of us are initially drawn to outward appearances and therefore, give utmost weightage to our external appearance. So if that is the key to making you love yourself, pamper yourself.

You are worth every bit of it. But again, this stuff only makes up the external part of you, while there is a lot more to your personality. If the above suggestion does not work for you, probably you could alternatively opt for encouraging yourself by stating simple and short sentences mentally or aloud, especially sentences implying what you would like yourself to be, in the future.

Focus on short sentences that you can easily form.

I am beautiful.

I am smart.

I am confident.

I am Intelligent.

I am happy.

I am a loving person.

I value myself.

I love my green eyes.

I love my lovely thick black hair on my head.

I love myself.

I love my life.

Focus on your positive attributes, qualities and areas and discard anything negative that comes to mind. Begin with short sentences. It will be a lot easier, and with time, your mind will start accepting your thoughts and your words, and you will begin to gradually love yourself.

Learn to love yourself. Accept yourself with your flaws and strengths. Care for yourself. You are you.

You are special, you are unique, and there is only one person who is you. Go right out and practice self-love every moment because people are going to treat you the way you treat yourself. If you are going to love yourself, then the world is going to love you.

Look at yourself in the mirror. Analyze yourself. Be realistic with yourself. Are you satisfied with what you see? If you are, then I must say you are doing great. If you are not satisfied with what you see in the mirror, then you must do whatever you need to, with the intention of making things good enough for you.

If you think you are overweight, do start with some basic exercising, running, stretching, taking the stairs instead of the lift or hit the gym. Whatever makes you happy and whatever is convenient for you should be initiated.

If you have unclear skin, then revisit your diet chart and drink lots of liquids. If you are not happy with your appearance, and if you think you need a makeover, do it. Let nothing in the world stop you. You got to do what it takes you to make things right for you.

I have seen people who are very confident in their skin asking the most apparent question that surfaces in their mind, "Why can't anyone accept me just the way I am?" I agree. However, let's just face the facts, for once. If you have expectations, so does the other person who is seeking you. Right? If you want the best, let's also ensure that we project our best selves in our best form too.

Often, it's the physical factors that pose the primary problem and the sooner the problem is taken care of, we are able to move into the preparatory mode.

So love yourself blindly because Love is the most powerful energy in the Universe. Having done that, do get to work, folks!!! Your time begins now...

3. LIST YOUR STRENGTHS

Once you have decided on whatever changes you want to make with the intention to feel positive or at least, you have chalked out your positive traits that match the newly emerged positive person that you are now, the first hurdle is overcome. You are worth a pat on your back.

It's very important to realize your strengths and positive characteristics because before you write, you tend to think and by thinking, you are also gaining clarity on your thoughts about your own self. Writing down also helps you to be clear about yourself, and thus, you ought to write even the traits that you have conveniently tossed into the backburner of your mind as 'absolutely impossible.' Yes! True! How can I be beautiful? Right?

Let's take an example. In case you consider yourself to be overweight or fat and cannot bring yourself to write that you are thin or slim although that's what you dream to become someday, it is fine.

Instead, you can opt to write, "Wow! I am so happy and grateful to see myself fit into a large or medium size outfit," as compared to the double-XL size that you are probably

12

wearing, at the moment.

You could alternatively write simple sentences like, "I am so happy and grateful that I am 55 kilos (or 121 lbs) now."

Think of as many positive attributes as you can and also change the not-so-positives that are already cemented in your mind into strong positive notes in your read-out list. By doing so, you no longer consider those as negative attributes. Instead, you have begun to give them a positive impact. It's wonderful to know that you have begun to scale up.

4. USE A MIRROR

Now that you have listed your awesome qualities and made a note of it either mentally or on paper, you have cleared the initial hiccup. Those of you who are absolutely lazy or some of you who cannot bring yourselves to write down on paper for whatever reasons, but have acknowledged your thoughts mentally, you too have done fairly well. As for those who are eagerly waiting to make a whole lot of changes in their lives, you have acquired some clarity on at least a few points, to begin with. Thinking and penning it down tends to bring about clarity in your thoughts.

I recommend that you start speaking aloud every line which specifies your positive traits in front of the mirror, preferably in odd numbers, like once a day or three times a day or five times a day or seven times a day and so on. The number of times you say a whole lot of good things about yourself, in front of the mirror, must be in odd numbers. It has worked well for me. So you could surely give it a try.

I am not saying you will immediately feel like you have turned beautiful as soon as you admit it in front of the mirror or you will become as slim as a model, the minute you say it

14

aloud, facing the mirror. No! Not at all! But the constant repetition of these words would slowly register in your subconscious mind and gradually make a change in you, and you would begin to notice that you are gradually turning out to be what you are proclaiming before the mirror.

Besides, the odd number of times that you practise saying good things about yourself, every time you pass a mirror anywhere, be it on the street, in a shop or anywhere, don't fail to appreciate yourself at least on a one-liner basis. For example, "Wow! I look amazing!" or "Wow! I am so happy and grateful to look so slim!" or "I am so happy and grateful to have such an amazing life!" You can begin with appreciating yourself, but then with time, do add some more areas of your life like your health, wealth, relationships and other areas that you need to improve upon.

The list can be as short as you wish or as long as you desire. What is important is that it has to be clear with comparatively short sentences. I have quoted some examples below for your reference.

A sample list:

About Me

1) I am so happy and grateful that I have clear skin.

2) I am so happy and grateful that I am slim.

3) I am so happy and grateful that I am 55 kilos (or 121 lbs).

Thank you, Thank you, Thank you, Universe.

About My health

1) I am so happy and grateful that I have perfect health.

2) I am so happy and grateful that my blood test is perfect.

3) I am so happy and grateful that I have a healthy heart which functions perfectly.

Thank you, Thank you, Thank you, Universe.

About My relationship

1) I am so happy and grateful that I have an amazing man in my life.

2) I am so happy and grateful that my partner and I have a blessed relationship.

3) I am so happy and grateful that my partner and I share a joyful, harmonious and a fun-filled relationship.

Thank you, Thank you, Thank you, Universe.

The most important part is that you should say "Thank you"

a minimum of three times, preferably after every sentence, or after all the sentences of a particular heading or area is done with.

5. IT ALL STARTS WITH YOUR MIND

The most important thing you have to realize is the potential of your mind. It can achieve just about anything and everything you want. It can manifest whatever you desire. There is no word called 'impossible' when it comes to manifesting what you want because all you need to do is truly use your mind, which is also known to be your most powerful tool. You must begin to train your mind to retain positive thoughts and sieve aside the negatives ones so that they don't prove to be a hurdle in your manifestation process.

There are sceptics who refuse to believe that the mind has the ability to achieve anything and everything that you desire. Instead, they tend to conveniently leave most things to fate. To make matters worse, today's chaotic lifestyle further complicates the problem. The apparent lack of time contributes to a defeatist outlook in response to any problem that arises in our lives and we tend to consciously or subconsciously accept the problems one after the other, until our thoughts get cemented with the firm belief *"Why me?"*

You can change that pattern of thinking. You can attain everything you desire, but at the same time, it does not mean that you are attracting someone else's share of food, money, luck or luxuries. It means that there is abundance all around you which is more than enough for everyone. You have the ability to attract whatever you wish or desire by applying your mind. Remember that everything that you see in this world has first been conceived in the mind in the form of a thought before it is manifested in reality. You need not be concerned about the source or the ability of the Universe to deliver.

You need to decide, believe and have undoubted faith in achieving whatever you have asked for. You need to have an enhanced awareness of what you wish to attract in your life, be it money, relationship, fame or happiness. You should also have a deeper unwavering faith and understanding that you can achieve it merely by putting your mind to it. You are already blessed with the creative power to create your life. All you have to do is to put it into use.

For example, after being in a relationship for 10 years with Ritesh, one day, after a bitter fight, Suma could see it all crumbling down.

19

Ritesh had broached the topic to his parents, stating his intention to marry Suma. All hell broke loose as his parents refused point-blank to accept Suma, at any cost, and made life impossible for Ritesh, who couldn't take a firm stand. Being the only son, he was hesitant to go against the wishes of his parents and on the other hand, his heart wouldn't let him break the relationship with Suma altogether.

Suma came across a video on social media in which some Indian spiritual leader spoke on the power of the mind. Intensely determined, she decided to set her mind on the task of getting married to Ritesh. During every possible break at work, all she did was imagine getting married to Ritesh and friends congratulating her.

She made a decision that come what may, she was going to be Ritesh's wife. She began shopping for the wedding outfit, shortlisting jewellery online and checking out venues, all along, giving the Universe the sign that she is planning her wedding. From a streetside shop, she bought a mangalsutra (a black-beaded chain worn by married women on their neck as a symbol of marriage in India) and put it around her neck. She also bought a plain ring for her ring finger. She took pictures of herself adorned with the jewellery and photoshopped it. Then she created a picture of Ritesh standing beside her.

It appeared as if they were married. She looked at the picture whenever she could, as it was the wallpaper on her phone, laptop, in her cupboard, behind her bedroom door, behind the bathroom door, and almost everywhere. In her mind, she was already married to Ritesh.

She kept making positive statements like, "My husband Ritesh and I look so good together. Thank you, thank you, thank you, Universe (or God or whoever you worship). We have a wonderful life together. Thank you, thank you, thank you, Universe."

Within six months, they were married and Suma matched and looked as beautiful as the picture she had put up. The picture took the shape of reality and it was stamped in her memory. She had already seen the end result several times in her mind's eye.

Your life wasn't going the way you wanted it to, until now, and that was because you lacked the knowledge and belief that the power to change your life is in your hands. Nobody would have told you, therefore, you did not know. Now that you are aware that you can change whatever you want in your life for the better, you need to put it in to practice.

You must monitor your thoughts carefully. Initially, it might take some effort, but the continuous rigorous practice will result in making your wish a reality, something easily achievable in the long run.

We create our destiny and we have had this gift to be the creators of our own lives since time immemorial. Each one of us has this awesome gift within us. What differentiates us from each other is the process or method of using this valuable gift. The process that works for one might not work for the other. But whatever might be the process, the choices that we make in order to have a better relationship, to become rich, or to better any other area of our lives, are all made by us and governed by the Universal Law which works differently for different people. We need to make use of the Law, at a conscious level, with a dedicated effort so that we create more and more of whatever we desire to experience. Thus we are not only shaping our destiny but our will as well.

The key is the continuous use of your mind in a positive way on a day-to-day basis so that you form a rhythm, over a period of time, and ultimately, it becomes a part of your personality and thought process without much of an effort. You reach a point where nothing is impossible to achieve because anything and everything is possible and achievable in literally, all the areas of your life. So filter your thoughts and consciously make an effort to retain or think positive thoughts while discarding anything negative that comes to mind.

The Law of Attraction works on the principle of Quantum Physics. Quantum Physics implies that everything must be first created in the inner world. The inner world is reflected outwardly like a mirrored reflection. It is by divine design that as soon as you are in vibrational sync with your desires, it will materialize outwardly.

Once you have a clear understanding of the quantum process, manifesting anything you wish in the outer world should be a cakewalk. Create your inner world of thoughts and the physical world will come into existence, forming the template of your thoughts. How easy is it? It's truly easy. You just have to believe and remember to have it imprinted in your mind's eye. It works every single time!

6. SWEEP AWAY THE NEGATIVE THOUGHTS FROM YOUR LIFE

We might have spent all the years of our lives thinking, behaving, cursing and feeling sorry for ourselves and our destiny. Put an absolute stop to this pattern of thinking right away. Let me clearly emphasize that this is going to be a Herculean task in the beginning, because the easiest thing in life is to think negative. The easiest path is to easily opt for the worst outcome.

If you have been endorsing such a pattern of thinking, first and foremost, you will need to clear your mind of all negative thoughts. There can be a variety of negative thoughts. Some of them make you feel that you are not good enough or question your personality or confidence in life, or make you believe that "I can't do it" even before you try something out. Negative thoughts include doubts like "Why do I attract losers in my life?" or "I am too fat and ugly that no man would ever date me" or "Girls don't get attracted to me as I am not rich enough or good enough." Another negative question that pops up most of the time is "Why me?"

Many of us are extremely comfortable and often certain when it

24

comes to thinking the worst of any situation. You might have even noticed that some of us love to feel sad or feel pity with the kind of tough life that we face. Then there are certain others who are so ultra-sensitive about everything that they worry and cry for hours and days. The tears might make you feel a lot better each time you weep, but that's no solution. There is another lot who are helpless in every situation. They live like a zombie with no interest in life, because according to them, nothing ever works in their lives. In such a situation, the ultimate result is that you attract more negative incidents in your life where you get ample opportunity to feel sorry for yourself, cry for yourself or continue being helpless.

All these negative thoughts will never work in your favour. Instead, these thoughts will appear to be huge obstacles that come in the way of your dreams. So change your thinking process altogether. The lesser the negative thoughts in your mind the quicker is the process of manifestation of your desires.

My advice to you is to just go with the flow and not stress yourself out. Clear the clutter and adopt a diehard attitude to manifest your wishes. Eventually, all your dreams would show up right in front of your eyes… Simply allow Nature to take its course. Unbelievable, but true!!!

7. START MEDITATION

Meditation is another option when you are way beyond being able to control your thoughts. Well, there must be so many people out there who cannot control their mind or focus on one thought or any specific subject for more than a few seconds. So how would they meditate? Right? At first, when you start meditating, there would be a zillion things zipping through your mind at the speed of light and often you will be aware that you started with thinking something, and in a few moments, your mind has raced through so many topics that you have lost count of them, in the process.

Do not worry.

Sit in a quiet place that is free from any form of distractions. Turn off the music, cell phone and everything else that's likely to distract you so that you have absolute silence around you to enable you to get in the mood for meditation.

You can wear loose clothes but ensure that you are comfortable in them. Meditation need not have a defined posture but any posture that suits you fine should do. Your comfort is your priority when it comes to meditating.

People normally say that you need to be seated in the lotus

26

position but if you are uncomfortable, sit in the way that is comfortable for you. What is more important is the fact that you need to breathe deeply and relax.

To begin with, you can either focus on something in particular like your breathing or the spot between your eyebrows or a sensation in the body. This is done with the intention to continuously bring your attention back to the focal point, every time your mind wanders. You might also be aware of things happening around you while you meditate but you need not react to anything even if it gets your attention.

You can start by meditating for at least 3-5 minutes and increase the duration gradually. Even if you meditate for as little as 5 minutes, it doesn't matter, but what matters is that it has to be done regularly. Regular meditation does have its benefits and positive effects over a period of time. You can also play some soft meditative soothing music in the background, if you prefer.

Just a few minutes of meditation everyday can bring you huge benefits. You can acquire excellent health, develop great positive feelings, attain an inner calm, improve your creativity, develop your ability to handle stress, and have the power to control your reactions, according to your will.

When you meditate, allow your thoughts to flow freely while

you keep your focus on the spot between your eyebrows and absorb your thoughts. Over a period of time, you will realize that you would stop having negative thoughts. You will begin to have good thoughts. Gradually, you can also start thinking of nothing.

Maybe, you can do what I normally do. I usually visualize a white light coming to me from the Sun which envelops me in a soft ball of warmth and abundant love. This light is like a protective ball around me. This light has the power to wipe away my negative thoughts, to help me handle stress more effectively, to get rid of my unhappiness and to make me calm, happy and mentally light enough to carry on my day, in the best possible way.

You can also do the same and you will feel energized, light and refreshed after your meditation process. You will feel like you are ready to face any external problem or issues with absolute ease.

In the event that you fail to meditate for a couple of days, for whatsoever reasons, be assured that the manifestation process would not come to a standstill. The process will slow down a bit and could probably take a longer time but it will happen. In the course of meditation, there is a point of time when your mind has no thoughts, it is not focused on anything in particular, and you might also see only plain lines or blobs of color... *During this phase, if you mediate with your goal in mind, you will achieve whatever it is you are aiming for.*

I too couldn't bring myself to relax and meditate at first, but once I began doing it religiously, there was no stopping me. I am aware of the power that meditation brought to my desires and my life. I am a changed person altogether and the good things that are happening in my life continue to happen every single day.

8. AFFIRMATION

Affirmations are stepping stones to what we wish to manifest. Yes! One needs to affirm constantly. This is another easy way to attract your desires. Affirmation is the repetition of words or sentences several times over. In order to affirm, you are required to write down your desired outcomes and act upon them. Have clarity in your thoughts, review what you want to focus on and envisage achieving whatever you yearn for.

Be careful about the words you constantly put into your mind. The words you read, repeat and focus on must be absolutely positive and only positive in nature. There is no place for anything that is negative.

This is another method that you can put into play which works very effectively if it is done with a feeling associated to it. Now simply imagine your desire, to have clear skin. How do you feel seeing yourself with a much clearer skin in your thoughts? I am certain you are elated, watching your smooth flawless skin.

Say it to yourself as a method of affirmation that you have clear, flawless skin. Repeat it a 100 times a day, "I have clear flawless skin." Keep doing this for a week or so. See the shift in your energy. Notice how you feel in a week's time. You will realise that you look far better, your skin is improving and you are beginning to like what you see in the mirror. You are happy seeing the better version of yourself. As you are emitting happiness, you will find more reasons to see your happiness increase besides the mounting confidence that affirmation works.

It gives you a boost. It makes you adopt a *'can do'* attitude. This attitude is a necessity in your journey to manifest your desires in your life. The 'can do' attitude will not allow you to give up easily. Affirmations help greatly, especially when people fail in adopting other methods of LOA.

Similarly, if you spend hours doing positive affirmations and then move on to making negative comments, the impact of doing the positive affirmations gets wiped off or lessened.

Continue being positive and avoid being negative in any way because negativity can really slow down or even wipe out the chances of your desires manifesting at all.

When you do affirmations, the key is to repeat them as

often as possible. Try and keep them as short as possible so that you can do it conveniently anywhere and anytime.

9. IMAGINE

The magic that this powerful tool brings along is unbelievable. Don't fret that you might not be able to manifest what you dream of. Everyone will be able to attract whatever he or she wants because the minute you think of anything on a continuous basis, it takes the form of reality, be it good or bad. It's already in the ready form. You need to match the frequency or vibration with the aim of drawing it into your life.

Manifestation happens when your vibration matches what you want. Whatever you want is already in existence. Thus, when your vibration is in sync with what is already in existence, you will attract it into your life. The power of manifestation primarily rests in your subconscious mind.

Your conscious effort to manifest anything is, by and large, a small percentage.

For instance, you decide that you wish to attract a fancy house for yourself. The effort that goes into consciously attracting it is for a very small period of time, say for 5 to 10 minutes or for a maximum of an hour. One hour of conscious attraction might present you with numerous other distracting thoughts gaining control besides the fancy house. So the one hour might not possibly be dedicated solely for manifesting and attracting your fancy house.

Over a period of time, after you have learnt to exert control over your negative or stressful thoughts, release the negativity so that you can begin the process of visualizing the dream life you always wanted. The negativity here is your doubtful ability to attract it in reality or the lack of money to attract the fancy house or certain old thoughts that are rooted deeply in your mind-set. For instance, the thought, "My parents worked hard all their life and barely made it through life, then how can I make it big in life?" You are different. You have a different life path to live. You are the creator of your life and your life is different from that of your parents. Your thoughts must therefore, be different from your parents too. Isn't it?

Visualize, see every detail of your dream life in your mind's eye, feel it and be happy seeing the outcome materialize as if it's happening for real.

You can include visualization in your meditation or you could alternatively do it repeatedly when you have the spare time to practise. What I have experienced is that visualization works at its best for me just before I go to bed. Often, if you visualize your dream life when you are almost on the verge of sleeping, you are powerfully attracting it to you.

Well, you will be a little surprised as one of my friends, Meena, applied the Law of Attraction by using it in the weirdest way I have ever heard of.

Meena is an exemplary case of how the Law of Attraction truly works. She is in a harmonious relationship for the last two years that's going great for her with only one major hurdle appearing every time she and her partner choose to be intimate. She tried on various perfumes, sexy clothes and scented candles, but in vain. Her man would never go down on her and she was too shy to ask him to do it. She was getting desperate to sort out this issue as this was turning into a major obstacle in their relationship and in the lovemaking act. One fine day, in sheer frustration, she asked out aloud to God for help to resolve her predicament without any embarrassment.

A few days later, she was gifted a book which spoke about the Law of Attraction. She disliked reading but flipping through some random pages, the power of visualization caught her attention and she decided to put it into test. She kept practising visualization for a couple of days. Lo and behold, the next time Meena made out with her partner, he went down on her without her asking or without any provocation from her end.

She was too stunned for words. She started giggling, leaving him wondering at her reaction. From that day onwards, she never had to ask ever. It just became the norm every time they made love. She is convinced that the Law of Attraction works.

Just like Meena is convinced, you too will be, once you are done with your litmus tests.

Chalk out your desires and give them images … like the car you plan to drive or the house you desire to live in or the dream-like relationship you are already living every day.

Let these dreams be crystal clear in your thoughts, down to the color of the car or the logo or emblem displayed on the steering of the car or the hug exchanged with your partner. Imagine how beautiful the car looks, parked in the driveway of your house.

Visualization, if done properly, cannot go wrong. Here the proper method is refraining from doubt or entertaining any contradicting thoughts.

For instance, do I want a red or a black or a blue car? Well, you got to be clear before you get into the act of making your imagination a reality. Clarity of whatever your heart desires has to be in sync with your mind.

If it's a relationship you are hell-bent on attracting, then visualize what it's like when you see them face-to-face and when you wake up every day besides them. Imagine what you feel when you smell the aroma of their scent, see them smiling at you or look into their eyes, and feel it. Feel that they too find you irresistible like you find them. Do this for a month or two and see the results. Check your emotions. They are powerfully happy. You are overjoyed beyond words.

During your visualization process, imagination is the key. So imagine whatever you wish, imagine the relationship, imagine the promotion, imagine the wedding and imagine whatever you want but imagine it with clarity and absolute vividness so that you feel as if it is happening in reality. Bask in the happiness. Be assured that the outcome is the reflection of your clear imagination. Nothing must deter that knowledge.

Most of us begin to apply the Law of Attraction by attracting small things; like I attracted an eagle on a Sunday. I then moved to attracting travel holidays, dinner dates, expensive clothes, and turning into a writer and so on. What I consistently noticed is that the Law of Attraction grew with each time I attracted what I wanted, and I got more and more confident. Now I am in the mind- set that mirrors the belief that nothing is impossible.

The latest instance was being a borderline diabetic to becoming perfectly fit with no medication in any form. I truly believe that all you need to do is, "Ask and you shall receive." It is as simple as that!!!

10. DECLARATION

Declarations must be positive. Positive Declarations! Positive Declarations! Positive Declarations!

When it comes to every desire that you would wish to manifest, firstly, you need to be very clear and certain about what you really want before you make any declaration. You come across many people who want something today, and change their mind about it tomorrow, and chase another thing the day after and so on. This gives out mixed signals. And mixed signals bring forth mixed results.

For example, Deepak had a perfectly running car and he liked it a lot although there were times he would complain about certain aspects of the car like, "It is quite outdated, so I want to get rid of it" or "It is not a great model anymore, so I want to get rid of it" or "I am fed up with this car as I have been using it for over 3 years, so I want to get rid of it." He would irrefutably declare the occasional drawbacks of a perfectly running car and also announce that he wants to get rid of it, little realizing that he was attracting everything that he was declaring.

39

He decided to pick up an additional car for the family. However, the moment he began checking out new cars, what came to his notice is that his current car started giving him too many technical problems that were cementing his earlier opinion of getting rid of the car, even more firmly.

Although he kept frequently declaring the adverse condition of the car, in a short time, it took the shape of 'constant complaining.' Although he kept bickering about the car, he didn't have any serious plans to sell it off. But with the recurring problems cropping up one after the other, he opted to sell off the car to his friend, Mahesh, and pick up a new one altogether.

What's astonishing is that he sold it off for a throw-away price to Mahesh, who was fine with all the problems that this car had as he couldn't possibly afford a brand-new car.

Despite selling off his car, Deepak was expecting to hear complaints about the car anytime soon but as he heard none, he decided to call his friend and inquire about the condition of the car.

The friend assured him that he is extremely happy and grateful being able to afford a car, in the first place. He then went about declaring that the car is fantastic and that he loves driving it. He got all the problems pertaining to the car fixed and it has been in an excellent condition since the last six months. This clearly showed that the old car has been doing great with the new owner, who was grateful that he could at least own a car.

I have cited this example because if you are checking out anything new, then kindly refrain from criticizing, or in other words, picking faults, or being ungrateful, while you are referring to your old stuff, unless you absolutely do not want it anymore. Whatever your focus is on, you tend to attract more of it. So do you wish to highlight the negatives in something? If you do, you would be getting more reasons to complain. You get exactly what you focus on. Hence, be very careful where you intent to invest your energy.

As you are clear on what you desire, you need to declare it to the Universe. You can set a deadline or put a date around the desire to see if the event or desire materializes. Having done that, you have to believe that what you asked for is going to happen. This belief has to be absolute with no scope for doubts.

For instance, Rita was unhappy about a proposal her

parents brought forth. She attempted to turn it down on several occasions but her decision was not acceptable to her parents. The boy was her father's best friend's son. Rita didn't seem to like the guy at all.

She found him to be drastically different from her in literally, every aspect of life. Whenever they communicated on the phone, Mark triggered some forceful political opinions, consistently resulting in arguments arising between them. He loved politics and was rather passionate about his preferences and would rashly react if Rita had to voice anything remotely different from his opinion. Rita also found Mark to be very immature and short-tempered with no respect for any of her views or opinions. No matter how hard she tried convincing her father about Mark, it fell on deaf ears.

She tried reasoning with her mother but her mother insisted that the guy was well-settled and so she must go for it. She knew this relationship was already creating havoc in her life and she was very unhappy about it but she continued speaking to Mark as that was what her parents wanted her to do.

Finally, one day, absolutely frustrated and unhappy after

having a short conversation with Mark when they had another argument over trivial matters, she declared aloud, "Good God, if Mark and I are not suited for each other, let this relationship die a natural death as soon as possible." She continued to declare this for the next couple of days.

Gradually, she noticed that Mark got busy and wasn't available to talk to her as frequently as he did before. In a month's time, he was almost non-existent in Rita's life. Mark had changed his mind about her. He seemed to find another girl interesting at the work place. She didn't have to do anything from her end to break off this relationship as her parents got a wind of it and let it go. She was relieved and thanked God several times.

The above example shows that it is important to declare your intent clear and aloud. Shout it out to the Universe in a clear, firm and strong manner once or several times or all day long. It is your choice. Declarations help you in sticky situations where you can't get out of the problem. This is one of the best ways to connect to the Universe, and as usual, the Universe never fails you!!!

11. WHERE IS YOUR VISION BOARD?

It is quite common for most of us to make resolutions, decisions and goals and go back on them. It is also not uncommon to break routines, to suit your individual convenience. This often happens because of the lack of time, stress factor, other work pressures, being lazy, or at times, the very fact that you doubt the sanity of the practices you adopt to attract your wishes and make them a reality.

Don't doubt. Try a small test, each time you think you are being silly and you are doing or following something equally silly to get your life on track. Try imagining your lover say something that you are eager to hear, or imagine receiving a gift from someone or attracting something trivial.

I would like to cite the example of Megha, who made a vision board pasted with lots of pictures, less than two months before her wedding. She wanted to look beautiful on her wedding day. So she went ahead and put up pretty faces of attractive women who resembled her from certain angles. She shortlisted the pictures of the same woman adorned in heavy clothing and jewellery, resembling the look of a bride and placed the pictures on her vision board. On some of the figures, she chopped off the head and pasted her face in place of theirs.

Besides wanting to look beautiful on her wedding day, her goal was to look slimmer by losing 10 kilos.

Due to her extended work hours, the only exercise she was able to do was walk to the bus stop, rather than taking a cab from her house, on her way to work. She also opted for the stairs, instead of the lift at the workplace. Her last alternative was a short walk after dinner that didn't seem to have a profound effect on her weight anyway.

She ran short of time and that was a major constraint but she religiously went about with the affirmations, declarations and visualizations, every night after work.

With less than a month left for her great day and her work load increasing, as she had to complete her deadlines before her much sought-out wedding break, her night walks after dinner took a back seat.

She often came home late and was unable to take a walk as she was too tired. However, she continued practising the methods of the Law of Attraction while lying on her bed at night until she slept off. The vision board was the inspiration to do it.

One evening, on her way back from work, she ate golgappa (an Indian savoury consisting of fried puff-pastry balls filled with spiced mashed potatoes, spiced water and tamarind juice) from a roadside eatery. She spent the next two to three days having an upset stomach. She worked from home and tried her own medication. She kept drinking ORS and barely ate anything except rice and Indian lentil porridge. In a few days, she felt better but continued with liquids, salad, yogurt and Indian porridge.

She recovered.

With a few days left for her wedding, she had to alter her wedding attire a little bit here and there. She anxiously checked her weight and realized that she had indeed lost 9 kilos in total from the day she had put up her vision board, stating she wants to lose 10 kilos.

On her wedding day, Megha looked radiant and much beautiful than the woman on her vision board. She admits, she lost weight without much effort from her end.

Although she didn't ask to fall sick, she considers it a boon to have lost 9 kilos miraculously and in time for her wedding. She was convinced the Law of Attraction worked in her case without causing her any major problems.

If you are convinced about achieving whatever you set your mind on, there is nothing that can stop you anymore. Your next focus must be to make a vision board, something like a collage with all your dreams pasted on it, in the form of images. Make it colorful, let it be exciting to look at, let it be motivating enough for you to read the lines penned down on your board and most importantly, keep it right where it catches your eye and attention.

Put up words and pictures and read it a couple of times, and meditate or imagine that each and every thing you have asked for on your vision board has already materialized. In your mind's eye, if you are happy seeing your dreams turning into reality, let's capture your happiness in reality too. Let's see you leap into the air, scream out in sheer happiness, and jump up and down in blissful joy.

Express it every way you can. After all, it is happening for real in your thoughts. It won't be far from happening in reality!

12. LOOK FOR CLUES

You have asked the Universe to fulfil your desires. You have also started to meditate on your desires. You have also begun the visualization process. Some of you may ask, "With all these efforts put in, how will people know if it's working for them?"

You will know.

You need to start looking for clues. Start observing everything all around you as the clues will start appearing and you don't want to miss them. At times, there will be ways the Universe indicates to you that the manifestation process has begun. Many people mistake it for a coincidence or take it for granted.

Let's hypothetically consider that you are in love with a guy called John who was your classmate but is based in Canada as of now, while you live in London. You have asked the Universe to bring John into your life and have declared a particular date. Your interaction just fizzled out and underwent a natural death when he moved his base to Canada. Maybe, the distance played a role and you both drifted apart.

48

You start off and follow most of the steps mentioned above. With the passing of time, you will start hearing or seeing John's name surface every now and then. That's an indication from the Universe that whatever you are asking for is within arm's reach.

You might, all of a sudden, come across an article where the name of the person is John. You might find an advertisement with the name John. You might watch a movie and get to know that the hero is called John or some character in the movie is called John. It is likely that you may, at times, also hear stuff about John from a common friend or you may come across incidents relating to the place that John belongs to.

Names, places or things would surge up out of nowhere and remind you about John. The frequency of such incidents that remind you of him would increase and keep popping up literally, all the time. Suddenly, Canada might catch the fancy of many people around you in their conversation or make headlines in the newspaper or Canada would come up more frequently in your conversation, unlike before. Basically, too many things relating to your friend John would catch your attention which wasn't the case before you began practising the Law of Attraction.

When these types of incidents keep occurring on a regular basis, you need to know and believe that the Universe is working to make your desires come true.

Similarly, if it's a car you want, you will begin to see it more often. You will spot it in magazines or in reality. You will begin to hear about your desired car from friends or see it on the television.

Some people will experience seeing numbers like 111 or 11:11 which is an indication that you are aligned to your desires. You might see it in the most unexpected places, at times, but nevertheless it's an encouraging sign that things are working in your favor.

Some of you might see signs in the form of certain things like a feather or a butterfly or a bird or a rainbow as your lucky omen. For some of you, it stems from past experiences. Seeing such things might be associated with a happy feeling, as if something good is on its way and the same applies here as well. Like for me, it's an eagle. Whenever I see an eagle, something good is sure to happen in my life. Lastly, it's a sure-shot indication that the Law of Attraction is working for you if you see increased synchronicity. People who can help you or guide you to manifest your desires will also appear out of nowhere.

All this only proves that the Law of Attraction is beginning to work on your case.

I would like to bring up the incident of Sheila. She had asked the Universe to give her a certain amount of money and had enthusiastically put up one particular amount of her choice on her vision board. She wasn't too happy with the handwriting, so she put up a new one with the same amount and pinned up the old one towards one of the corners of the board, not wanting to dispose it as yet. A month later, she got a message on her cell phone from the bank stating that an amount similar to her request on her board has been credited into her account. The amount credited was a total of the old and the new amount written on the vision board.

She read the message on a Tuesday morning and the first thought that came to mind was that the bank had made a mistake.

Within the next couple of days, a number of bank executives called her, asking if she would be interested in opening a fixed deposit with the bank as she could earn some fairly good interest rates on her existing money. She was taken aback because as per her knowledge, she hardly had any money in her account to even barely sustain. So she responded saying that she did not have any money to put away into a fixed deposit that earns her some extra amount. She got her first clue in the form of a message, yet she failed to recognize it.

What I want you to note here is that these calls from the bank executives were another indication or clues from the Universe that Sheila's desire was fulfilled.

Well, on Sunday morning, she did get a weekly consolidated message on her cell phone stating that her account balance stood at a new astonishing total. On receiving this message, she felt the nudge and hurried off to the nearest ATM. She withdrew a small amount, yet the balance matched the morning message on her cell phone that she had received from the bank.

She understood.

She just knew with every fiber in her body that her request has been granted by the Universe. She literally started jumping in the ATM center and when she stepped out of the ATM center, she met the surprised glances of people waiting in the line outside the ATM, while some others had a broad smile plastered on their face and certain others stared at her as if she had gone out of her mind. But she knew with absolute conviction that the Universe had delivered what she asked for.

Nothing could stop her enthusiasm or confidence. She felt on top of the world, and said aloud to random people standing in the queue, "I love MY life!"

It is a different story that she refused to lay her hands on the money for another three months, until the accounting year ended as she was sceptical about this money being solely hers, where she actually had the freedom to use it as and when she pleases.

Although Sheila's request was fulfilled within the same month, her rational mind did take a whole week to come to terms with it and another three months to begin to use the money which was hers. She stated that she had not been checking her account lately for two reasons. Firstly, she was not expecting the Universe to give her the money so quickly and secondly, she was not keen to check her account details as her bank balance was showing an all-time low for the last three months before she asked for the money.

That is the complexity of being a person who thinks rationally.

This kind of a reaction is quite common at the initial stages of applying the Law of Attraction. Hence, it is natural that such doubts and fears will arise, but you need to believe and remember that the Universe undoubtedly delivers every wish, every single time you ask for it.

Each time you receive a clue or sign, be happy and remember that you have set the ball rolling...

13. BE GRATEFUL

The followers of most religions thank God for the food they eat, even before they actually eat it. They thank God in advance for the food. They do it to show that they are grateful for the food for the day.

Many of us use the phrase "Thank you" in our day-to-day life. This is one of the forms of expressing the feeling of gratitude. You cannot keep getting more and more of what you want if you are not thankful for what you already have. Gratitude is a very powerful method of exercising the Law of Attraction

The feeling of gratitude itself makes your life magical. So begin your day with being grateful or thankful for the day itself. You can start by being thankful for one more day that you live on planet Earth itself. You can be grateful for this amazing planet and the existence of all the species. You can be grateful for your perfect health which enables you to see, to think, to feel, to touch, to taste, to hear and to experience the awesome creations of planet Earth in every possible way. You can be grateful for your perfect relationships around you. You can be grateful for the never-ending flow of money. You can be grateful for all the happiness and experiences that you have had a chance to access.

You can simply start being grateful for everything. Say "Thank you" for everything, even for the ability to think and form your sentences.

Make gratitude a practice. Inculcate it in your thoughts, actions and let it flow into every vein of your bloodstream. Over time, you will notice drastic changes in your life. You will notice great reasons to smile and be happy. Never miss out on a single opportunity to be grateful or to say "Thank you." You can say it openly or in your mind or to the person. The most effective way is telling a person "Thank you" by meeting his or her eyes. The impact is almost magical if you sincerely mean and say "Thank you." What's important is that you feel the power of gratitude when you say it.

Say "Thank you" a hundred times in a day and see how your energy level shoots up. Your life can only get magical with these beautiful words. *"Thank you."*

The more you use them the more magical your life will be.

14. FEEL GOOD NOW AND ALWAYS

You can ask for the sun, moon and stars but before you do that, ask yourself, whether you are ready and feeling great from within to receive it.

Many of you must have asked for that perfect relationship in your life but then, are you happy enough and willing to rub off your happiness on someone special or would you gladly bog your partner down with your sad, negative, unhappy, pessimistic nature and thoughts?

If so, then even if you attract a loving relationship, it is doomed forever. Seek what you wish for within yourself before you seek it in others. If you are unhappy, you can never make another person happy. Your inner self is a reflection of your outer reality.

Well, this reminds me of another beautiful example. While travelling on a flight, you often meet the airhostess who makes an announcement regarding the 'dos and don'ts' to be practised where your safety is concerned. She clearly points out that in case of an emergency, before you help another, first fasten your oxygen mask and fasten your own seat belt and decide only later to do it for another person. In other words, you are the primary source in every situation. If you are safe, you can go about saving others. Similarly, if you are happy, you can go about making others happy.

You got to start feeling good now and continue with feeling good always as there is no downtime when it comes to attracting what you desire. You have to be in a vibrational alignment now and always to attract your desires.

What you are within is what you reflect to the outside world. If you are happy within, trust me, your eyes would sparkle with happiness, your smile would be radiant and over a period of time, your face would radiate such a youthful beauty that would defy your age for sure.

You have to be in a high vibration or a feeling of deliberate happiness to get what you have asked for. So I would advise you to seek happiness in the smallest occurrences and incidents. Give yourself reasons to rejoice, laugh and be grateful. Every time you ask for something, you must aim to put yourself in a state of absolute happiness in order to receive it.

There might be instances when you will be tempted to be a part of the office politics or gossip, especially about someone you strongly dislike or do not get along with. You might be tempted to go about narrating your sob story and you might be feeling sorry and unhappy about your life, and at times, go from person to person, narrating it to gain sympathy from them. But such behavior further gets you to a really low vibrational point and away from the manifestation of your desires. This is your reality 'in the now.'

Hence, it's very important to refrain from indulging in such activities. Instead, you must learn to ignore the negative incidents occurring in and around you. If you are unable to bring yourself to do it, then you could try to focus and be happy for so many things that you already have in your life. The vibration will automatically increase exponentially.

If you don't have any reason to be happy, just be happy for your five amazing sensory organs that have given you an opportunity to see and know yourself, feel the awesome sensations that exist, taste the most exotic food prepared, hear your favorite music created, smell the most attractive flowers and Nature after the first rain or anything that you find worth reminiscing about.

Often, your surroundings include people around you who could make you feel low, and prompt you to think negatively. You need to break off from them. Get away from them. You need to charge yourself with several extra dosages of positivity, gratitude and happiness, thus raising your vibrations, and allowing life to present you with the best.

There are people who visualize and think happily for a certain period of time, especially if they are trying hard to attract something in their lives. After a few days of attempting, if the outcome fails or there is a delay in manifesting, these people are back to bickering and complaining and being unhappy throughout the day. They return to being their true selves. If you are doing just what these people do, then do yourself a favor. Please do not ask yourself, "Why is it that my desires are not manifesting?"

The Universe loves to grant every wish you ask for. The Universe loves speed and wants to fulfil your wish at rocket speed. For this to occur, you have to put yourself in a really high vibration filled with positivity and happiness enveloping you so that you make it easy for the Universe to deliver your wishes at rocket speed, the moment you ask for anything.

Feel everything. Feel with feeling. Feelings are emotions. So feel with your heart. Feel excited. Feel like it's a dream come true when you see the end result of your visualization. Let it bring tears of joy to your eyes. Feel like it is happening for real, right in front of your eyes. If you lack the feeling aspect, then you are missing out on the most important emotional power pack that is instrumental in helping you create your desires in reality.

Just being hopeful is not enough. You have to harbour a crazy, passionate, burning, focused desire to see dreams manifest into reality.

If you aim to be a fashion designer, see it happening in the now. Feel like you are already a success and in no time you will discover innumerable paths to get you there. The Universe will open up infinite avenues for you to make it happen.

There is an example, I would like to cite here. Mayank was an avid follower of the Law of Attraction. As he was busy working the entire week, he usually kept aside every Saturday to do laundry work. On Sundays, he would have the ironing man, coming home and collecting his clothes. He worked with a multinational company in the sales department and lately, found himself travelling extensively on work-related purpose. So he was not able to do the laundry for over two weeks and the pile was too much to handle. Besides, he was running out on clean clothes to wear to work.

Literally, the entire week when he was back in town, it rained nonstop. Mayank was doubtful about being able to get his clothes washed and dried in the coming weekend as well. He had to get it done this weekend itself. Otherwise, the only option left was to shop for new clothes for work. It didn't appear as the perfect solution because he had another travel scheduled for the coming week.

He stopped thinking negatively about the entire scenario of laundry. He began to daydream that Saturday is a sunny day to the extent that he enjoyed the warmth of the sun on his skin as he made his way to a nearby restaurant for lunch. He imagined laying his hands on the warm and crisp dried shirts too. He continued feeling the warmth of the sun all through the day, imagining it to be Saturday although it was Friday and it was raining endlessly.

Early Saturday morning, the gloomy weather gave the impression of a likely downpour anytime. The weather could not deter him from being positive. He was very happy and confident that today was going to be a sunny day. He thanked the Universe for the sunny day which is happening in the now. He thanked the Universe for the hot blazing sun that has just come up now and went about getting his clothes washed in the washing machine, in spite of his roommate dissuading him from washing.

Mayank kept his thoughts intact and thanked the Universe several times for the scorching sun. He took a shower while his clothes were being washed. By the time his clothes were done, the sun was also up and warm against his skin, matching his imagination. He smiled and kept thanking the Universe for the sunny day as he spread his clothes on the cloth line. When he collected them in the evening, he thanked the Universe as soon as he felt the crisp and warm dried shirts with his hands.

Feel in the now... *Feel* happy now... *Feel* happy always.

15. ACT LIKE IT IS IN THE NOW

Another aspect is that if you have *asked* for the manifestation of your dreams, you need to *expect* it to manifest and be ready to *receive* it. You have placed a request to the Universe and accordingly, you need to trust the Universe to deliver it. You hold the belief that the Universe will fulfil your desires. Therefore, you have to be willing and open to receive your desires.

Once you put out a request to the Universe, I would advise you to go a step further and behave as if you have already received what you wanted. I understand perfectly that many of you out there would find it challenging to behave like your desire is fulfilled when you are still expecting or awaiting its manifestation. It might appear fake to many of you.

Nevertheless, just try and do it.

Pretend you have it already. Over a period of time, your mind will also accept it.

If you have asked the Universe for money, then learn to pretend like you have already received it. You must refrain from sending out a signal of lack or desperation. On the contrary, begin to spend money as if you are already living in abundance. Give away small amounts in charity. Spend on yourself. The above act indicates that you are already living the life of abundance. You are acting like it is in the now.

Monica had newly become acquainted with the concept of the Law of Attraction. She decided to test and see if it works and put forth a request for a free amount of money. She decided to pretend like she was living a life of Abundance. She behaved as if she had already received the free money she asked for.

It did cross her mind on a frequent basis as to who could possibly give her Rs. 50,000 without even asking for it, but she shoved her doubts away and decided to have faith and see the magic work for her. She shopped for fashionable clothes and visited fancy restaurants. She gave out the message to the Universe that she was already living in Abundance and had already received the money she had asked for.

Monica expected to attract the money in a month's time but it didn't happen. And like most people, she too lost interest in the practice but she continued living an abundant life which she had adopted while she was practising the Law of Attraction. She no longer focused her attention on attracting the free money she had asked for, as the manifestation didn't work for her within the deadline of a month that she had set. She concluded that the Law of Attraction doesn't work at all.

In the interim, she was being appreciated for her stylish clothes at work and in her personal life. With her spirits at the peak, the compliments further encouraged her to join dance classes as well as the gym in the hope of getting fit. She wanted to ensure she continued to turn heads as she was enjoying the new attention she was receiving ever since she had begun practising the LOA.

Although Monica started off this practice with the intent to test the certainty of the Law of Attraction and had adopted a pretentious act of living in abundance, she continued living the new lifestyle that still spelt abundance. She got into the habit of changing her wardrobe for the better, did better makeup and also bought matching shoes and jewellery. She was a new personality altogether.

Three months later, her CEO invited Monica to her cabin and gave her a check of Rs. 1, 00,000 (1Lac) for saving a large amount of money for the organization. She had hired the manpower required by the organization much before time, thus making a huge profit for the company.

The company had decided to reward her for her performance.

She was stunned. She realized that the LOA works. It gave her more than she asked for but it took time because of her uncertainty. Occasionally, she would ponder on who could give her free money and rack her brain, thinking about it for a considerable amount of time, which proved to be a setback, in a way. It delayed the process though it indirectly paved her path to still continue the abundant life she was living when she was practising the LOA.

Monica was aligned to the frequency of receiving the same.

The very act of having anything you desire 'in the NOW' brings it into existence and into reality. You are no longer waiting for it to happen (futuristic) so that you can be happy because every time you are waiting for it to happen, you tend to send out a signal of not having it as YET, and therefore, you remain in a state of not having it as yet. The state of having your desire fulfilled, in essence, leaves you no longer in a state of need. You experience a condition of abundance.

People who have recently started to practise the Universal Law or the Law of Attraction would have to begin with smaller requests so that once your desires are fulfilled, you will develop more confidence and your belief in your ability to attract things will grow exponentially.

There are people who say that you need to ask for big things rather than waste precious time asking for small irrelevant stuff. Do not straight away try manifesting big dreams because they usually do not work or they take a long time unless you are truly in the mind-set of attracting it or you possess attributes that are already aligned to the same frequency as your desires or you are someone who has been a pro at attracting whatever you want.

Your constant doubts on whether it will materialize will only further delay the process of manifestation. So you need to take one step at a time, baby steps, if I may say. Once they manifest, you can move on to bigger desires and goals as that will give you the confidence that whatever you ask for with belief, will manifest.

There is another example that I would like to bring to light. My cousin, Sheeba, is a shopaholic who had a weakness for branded clothes, shoes, bags and accessories. However, over a tiff with her boss, she resigned in a fit of temper and remained unemployed for nearly two months. Her birthday was approaching and with a lot of idle time on her hands, she began browsing an online site for the latest fashionable clothes and chanced upon a very attractive suit. She took an instant liking to it. She knew this outfit was hers but found it too expensive to splurge money, being unemployed, at the moment.

The outfit was unaffordable then, and so Sheeba shelved the idea of buying it for the time being, resolving to pick it up as soon as she was employed.

In the interim, she clicked a picture of it and saved it on her phone and looked at it several times, unable to get her mind off the dress. The color, print, pattern, fall, material, everything was perfect. She just knew it was hers even without buying it. She imagined wearing it for her birthday and receiving many compliments. She kept thanking for the dress she owned. Although she didn't own it in reality, she knew it was hers.

With less than a week for her birthday and still unemployed, she wasn't willing to give up on the dress. She knew she would land a job someday but she would lose the dress to someone else if she didn't act on it. She made up her mind to buy the dress and promptly decided to use her credit card which would give her a payback time of a month for the dress.

As she shortlisted the dress and put it into her online shopping cart, a pop up on the screen appeared, mentioning she could avail a 10% discount on that particular outfit as proposed by the individual seller. She was so glad and kept thanking the Universe for saving a little of her money. As she was preparing to enter her credit card details, a screen shot appeared indicating that she was eligible for a refund from the online website that was higher than the cost of her dress.

Her past shopping had earned her eligibility points which came up in the form of money. She availed it. The balance amount remained in her online account. The dress came absolutely free of cost to her. Her happiness knew no bounds and she was jumping around in joy.

She could barely afford the dress, yet the Universe designed everything in such a manner that she wore it on her birthday just as she had visualized, for FREE!

Be in the now of things ... Start getting into the 'forever good' feeling. Just feel good always. Nothing should stop you.

I want to tell everyone that you need to live in the moment and enjoy everything around you always. Once you are in this alignment, you barely need to keep asking and reminding the Universe for anything because the Universe knows everything. You only have the responsibility to get yourself into a feeling good vibration now and always.

For instance, you can observe children around you. They have a carefree mind and you will notice that they easily get most of the things they wish for. They effortlessly attract it by their sheer love for it because they are almost always in sync with the vibration that matches their desire. It doesn't cross their mind to doubt if their desires would manifest.

Now notice an adult, who is reading about the Law of Attraction, practicing positive thinking and many other methods of the Law of Attraction, yet finds it difficult to attract simple things only because of an excess of knowledge which often contradicts his thought process. He spends too much time wondering how it can ever happen.

His rational thinking works overtime, confirming his belief that it just can't happen and each time he thinks so, his doubts keep mounting manifold... The end result ... Months pass and nothing happens. He begins to believe that such things don't exist.

So be childlike, awaken the child in you, because the Universe does not take time. Everything that you think already exists in actuality. Everything is already in the Now!

16. BE CAREFUL HOW YOU PEN DOWN YOUR DESIRES

We all know by now that the Law of Attraction and the Universal Laws are very powerful. In order to apply them in our daily lives, we have to consciously and intentionally use them.

You can get the best outcome from the Law of Attraction when you write down your dreams or goals. I am aware that for some of you, speaking is way easier as compared to writing, as there are so many people who are not confident enough to write things down and as a result, they hesitate to pen down their thoughts. You don't need to be a high school pass-out to write down your goals. The intention behind writing is not to ensure that your language is fancy or stylish, although some amount of grammar does play a role in what you write.

For example, you write a sentence like "I will be a successful person" or "I hope I can buy a house" or "I would like to see myself as a successful person someday."

The above sentences indicate that you might be a successful person but it will be somewhere in the future. There is a thread of uncertainty when it comes to manifesting. The process of attracting anything will take time. It might even take forever. It is definitely not around the corner, for sure.

While a sentence like, "I am a successful person," indicates that you already are a success. You are no longer waiting to be a successful person. There is a clear indication of already being in the now rather than in the future.

Merely thinking or speaking about your goals will also help but the degree of impact it has on your desires being fulfilled will be minimal and the manifestation process might appear to be a distant dream in certain cases. So I suggest, you write down what you wish to attract.

Journaling provides more clarity about your desires. Buy a diary or a notebook that appeals to you and start penning down your goals.

An average person tends to think approximately 70,000 thoughts per day. But none of the varied topics that you think of, throughout the day, has any kind of clarity because thoughts randomly move from one thought to another and so on.

In order to make your desires specific and precise, the most effective technique is writing. Writing is, in a way, training the mind to focus and concentrate on a particular subject until the subject is precise, detailed and crystal clear.

You could start by dreaming how amazing life would be if you had your perfect partner to spend your life with, in absolute bliss. The moment you have clarity of thought, capture it on paper. Your dreams won't take shape at the snap of your fingers. Some effort will have to go into it. However, the effort is simplified in your case by writing it down although when you read it, there is a likely chance that you might not be convinced, reading about an amazing life on paper. It appears to be too good to be true. In such a situation, you will have to set aside your fears and apprehensions and also everything else that tends to block your dreams from turning into reality.

I know a lot of people who appear as very successful. They have a fabulous job, look reasonably presentable, appear confident, smart and well-mannered and much more, but they are still single. After having all of the above, some of them tend to ask, "How come I am unable to attract even one person in my life for a date, while others have a rocking love life? Where am I going wrong?"

The process of finding a partner is the same for everyone, yet some of them find their partner very easily while others take years. Most women I know on planet Earth expect a fairy-tale experience or wish to be treated like a princess. But then where is prince charming? He doesn't appear out of thin air!

Define what you are looking for in your perfect partner. Yes, it is as easy as that. But then most people don't know what they want in their perfect partner. There are two sides to your definitions. What do you want in your partner and what you do not want in your partner!

You can start by jotting down what you want in your soulmate. You can be as specific as possible, right up to the eye color. The list can be as long as you want. I would suggest, you must factor in and note down every point that you can possibly think of. You are looking at something long-term and if this is your golden chance to order, so be it. You can't afford to be vague and miss out on something important that you might regret later. Be as precise as possible.

Also, be very careful what you ask for because the Universe never fails to deliver it.

Let's consider Petra's story. She was getting tired of the number of men she was dating as none came up to her expectations. She found most of them to be immature and some rather childish too. In case, she coincidently did find the mature man, he was surely taken.

She felt sorry for herself. She felt sorry she didn't think about marriage much earlier. She felt sorry she rejected most guys, who approached her during her youth, for no rhyme and reason. She felt sorry for the relationships she screwed up without a thought. In hindsight, she realized that one of her ex-boyfriends was indeed so good while she was not worthy of him. Too late! She couldn't reverse the situation to suit her as he was married and well-settled by then.

Tired of attracting the same immature guys with similar attributes, she got into making a list. This time her partner list was so long that it remotely matched the length of an Indian sari.

She carefully added this line in bold, "My partner makes time for me and he matches the maturity of a married man."

Her list done, Petra was all excited. She dutifully read her list every alternate night before heading to bed. She imagined sharing her bed with him, she felt her partner's love for her, and she dreamt how beautiful life would be with him. Soon enough, her dream man, Anton appeared and within six months, she was head over heels in love with him.

It was several months before the truth finally dawned on Petra.

Anton had a past relationship with Anna during his graduation and it didn't work out. He was heartbroken for over two years. He went into depression and almost ruined his career with his excessive drinking habit which ultimately landed him in the hospital when he began vomiting blood.

During that phase, he had a childhood friend, Debbi. She was actively involved with the day-to-day happenings in Anton's life, including the love story with Anna, which left him heartbroken. Coincidentally, Debbi too had come out of a broken relationship and was shattered for a year, resulting in poor academic results and several backlogs.

Anton, on recovering, decided to stay clear of girls forever and Debbi, after her poor results, took a vow never to fall in love and get hurt ever again.

Anton and Debbi decided to work hard and focus only on their studies. They cleared engineering after a year. Their friendship helped them to get out of the mess and carve a bright future for themselves.

On completing their engineering courses, both of them

secured jobs in different cities. Before they parted ways, they decided to cement their strong friendship forever in the disguise of being married.

Both of them were not interested in getting married to anyone else at all. They thought it best to get married to each other through a court marriage. They were not in love with each other and were convinced that as they were going to be separated from each other, it was best to be married temporarily to each other, which in turn, would prevent them from getting close to anyone else.

Over the years, they remained distant from each other. Now after six years, Anton met Petra and disclosed that he was in a namesake marriage. He considered himself single. As far as Petra was concerned, he was everything she asked for and he undoubtedly had the maturity of a married man, although, she didn't ask for a married man in the literal sense. Anton was a married man only on paper. Petra had no choice but to break it off for good as Anton would have to go through a divorce to be eligible to remarry, besides she had her doubts if Debbi would agree to a divorce, taking into consideration the low status divorced women had in India.

Even if Debbi were to agree, Petra's family would never

consent to her decision to marry a divorcee. However, she didn't have to struggle with the consequence of their relationship as Anton finally admitted that he cannot marry her, as Debbi was unwilling to go in for a divorce because it would pose a major problem when people realize that Debbi had a concealed marriage status already. In another six months, Anton and Debbi got married to each other publicly, for the sake of their families, pretending that it was an arranged match.

Petra indirectly got what she asked for. So here again, I am trying to point out that one needs to be very careful what one craves or asks for. Read your list several times and consider with care, if any sentence has a different connotation or meaning to it. If yes, change it immediately.

I am speaking from experience that the Universe never fails to give you whatever you ask for with absolute faith. So a word of caution, be very careful about what you ask for.

17. KEEP YOUR DREAMS A SECRET

Everybody has a dream. Likewise, everyone maintains a secret too. The wise decision here is that you must keep your dreams a secret. Not everything works for everyone. Something that works for someone need not work for everyone else. Therefore, it is advisable to keep things to yourself until it works out for you.

You must strictly keep your goals or dreams to yourself simply because the opinion of others has a tendency to influence your confidence and create doubts, and often disbelief in your ability to attract whatever you desire, especially if you are in the early stages of practising the Law of Attraction. Certain people's opinions are likely to come across as an obstacle in the manifestation process of your dreams. Besides, certain others might not really exhibit a positive vibe towards your dreams. And lastly, if you think you can't keep a secret, why expect others to keep your secret a secret.

Every person you meet might not be as happy for you as you are for your own self. They might not be as positive and energized as you are while practising the LOA. Any negative energy that comes your way can act as a hindrance and dilute the process of manifestation. Energy is put into manifesting your goal. So be cautious about the kind of energy that you are attracting by disclosing your innermost dreams, visions and goals.

The less experienced lot of people, who are still at the early stages of applying the LOA, must avoid discussing their desires with anyone at all.

Let's take the example of Priyanka.

Priyanka was absolutely new to following the LOA techniques but she was very excited to get going. She got all geared up and made a vision board with pictures of BMW pasted on it with affirmations stating that, "This blue coloured BMW is mine."

A few days later, she had her friends come over to her house for a party. Everyone looked around the décor of the house. They caught sight of the vision board and she was all ears to a mouthful from them that the next time certain friends visited her place, the vision board was no longer there. She had it removed forever. She no longer believed or followed it.

Can you imagine what would it be like when people who know nothing about such stuff see a board pinned up with fancy, colourful pictures and unbelievable statements displayed on it? Some of them would laugh and some of them would even take a step further and point out how absurd the entire stuff appears to seem. Certain others would openly declare that one must be out of their head to think that one could put up pictures of unattainable materialistic things he or she desires, and they would have the ability to manifest it in their life merely by doing such activities without any hard work.

The comments of her friends too mirrored the above and Priyanka was convinced that merely reading a book or changing one's thought pattern cannot attract wealth or a relationship or even a promotion for anyone. Just by pasting pictures on a board, you cannot get things done. But in reality, everything that Priyanka thought to be impossible is very much a possibility. There are millions of people who can vouch that they have attracted several unbelievable things in their life by applying the above principles.

Uncertainty is a part of anything that is new and there are high chances, you might still be harbouring some limiting beliefs within you, which will appear as an obstacle in the way of your manifestation process. In such circumstances, you will gain confidence only after something that you have asked for is fulfilled or something incredible happens. Once that happens, automatically your confidence level shoots up and you will eliminate the two worst emotions that cropped up all along, that is, FEAR and DOUBT. On knowing that you have the power to attract whatever you desire, you will realise that your destiny is in your hands and no negativity can possibly prevent your dreams from turning them into reality.

Your belief will be definite. So allow the Universe to magically manifest your dreams.

18. FREEZE YOUR LIST

Most of us go grocery shopping. Don't we? What happens when we do not list the items that we need? We tend to forget. Let's ensure this doesn't happen to us when we go shopping for a potential partner or a hubby dear or a home.

Attracting a partner does sound like jingle bells, all of a sudden, to my ears. Write down your list and get your partner! Yes, it is that easy but the crux here is that you need to do it right.

That's what Pinky learnt from her own experience.

She was a diehard romantic who would read nothing but *"happily ever after."* Immediately after her studies, she bagged a job. She met a dashing man at work and was absolutely smitten by him. She followed him, tracked him and spied on him like some investigator on a case. She did nothing else about it. In about six months, like others at work, she too received his wedding invite. The name on the card was Sonia.

She broke down crying. She had done nothing from her end to see her name reflect on the card. She had put in no effort, yet it broke her heart to see her heartthrob marry someone else. She had zilch idea that she could attempt to attract this man if she even remotely knew the 'how to go about formula' for the same, but she was only interested in reading romantic novels and putting nothing into practice.

His life had moved on and hers did too, eventually. Time flew and her age crossed swiftly from twenty-five to near mid-thirties. The years changed her life drastically. She was gifted a couple of spiritual and motivational books focusing on the power of the mind, positive thinking, LOA, yoga and many more aspects, as her birthday presents which she eventually began reading.

With every book she read, it was evident, romantic books took a backseat. She had graduated in her choice of reading!!!

One book led to another and she read about 150+ books in about two years. If only she had known that 'we create our destiny,' she would have attracted her dream man, much earlier. She mentioned that she had gotten her eyes opened to the several prospects that appeared within her reach, although in the bargain, it did confuse the hell out of her as well until it got her thinking of the most important question

...

"Where do I start?"

She wanted to attract a happy marriage with a wonderful man. She concluded that a "man that came slightly close to marriage material" was what she needed in order to get her tests going.

So she began to list down what she wanted in a partner and it ended up with about 32 points in total, out of which there were about three must-haves which would be an indicator to confirm that 'he is the one,' along with the other specifications like character, qualities, geography, chemistry, etc.

The three must-haves that she specified were, the first point being, she wanted him to be able to speak one foreign language besides English and Hindi.

Secondly, as she was black-eyed and was quite bored looking into them for the last thirty-four years, she eagerly looked forward to peer into a pair of beautiful brown eyes for a change. Lastly, not wanting to go through a surgical correction in order to acquire one of the most sought-after beauty enhancers called dimples for herself, she decided it should suffice if the man had a dimple on at least one of his cheeks!

Wow! She was excited as her list was finally ready after several changes. It was tough making her first list. She did go

86

back and forth on it several times with every happy and not-so-happy couple she came across. Her list would change several times. She would keep having more additions and some subtractions. This went on until she firmly decided to call it a day.

She had finalized it and promised herself not to change anything about the list. No matter how many happy couples she met, she believed that everything she wanted was already on her list. It made her life a lot easier that way. In a few months' time, she met men but nothing went beyond a date or a meeting or two and it would fizzle out. Once her list was finalized with no more corrections, she began religiously reading it every night and carefully tucking it under her pillow before she slept. In some time, she began meeting men who coincidentally matched certain qualities mentioned on her list but none proceeded beyond a few meetings.

A year later, unexpectedly, her car broke down on a highway and a smart looking, light-eyed man, called Gaurav came to her rescue. He was kind enough to keep her company until the guys from the service centre arrived to sort out the issue.

In the course of conversation, Pinky noticed his dimples flashing whenever he smiled and was smitten with his brown eyes as well. They exchanged visiting cards before he left and she didn't think much about it. A week later, Gaurav invited her for a drink and soon enough, they were in an exclusive relationship.

Meanwhile, Pinky had forgotten about her list and during one of her cleaning up chores, she discovered that Gaurav matched her list to the 'T.' She realized he had the three *'must-haves'* she had jotted down in her partner list. He had brown eyes, dimples and could converse in French too. Two points were missing from the rest of the list but it was irrelevant. Her magical list had come true. They got married in less than six months.

She was married after over a year of writing the list. The delay occurred because she was undecided for several months after writing down what she needed in a man, and this was the signal she was emitting to the Universe.

Each one of you got to explicitly express what you need in your list and quit making changes every now and then, because every change you keep making, will only delay the process and yield you confusing results. So be firm once you prepare the list!

19. REASON OUT YOUR LIST

Let's start with you being very clear about what you really want. I hear a lot of people saying that, *"I want a nice person as my partner"* or *"I want a roller coaster life."*

These sentences lack the depth in terms of clarity unless you tend to elaborate it a bit more. You need to describe what the term 'nice' means to you. Ask yourself what you mean by the word 'nice.' Why do you want him to be nice? What else would you want him to be, besides being nice? How do you want to be treated by your partner? Reason out your list.

You must elaborate on the description to ensure clarity on the aspects you want.

In the case of the above generic phrase "I want a nice person as my partner," you could explain the feel-good factor of the sentence. You could instead, write it in the following manner:

My partner appreciates me and asks for my opinion on most matters.

My partner is kind to me and creates opportunities to make

me smile and be happy.

My partner respects and appreciates me for what I am.

My partner makes me feel comfortable and loved always.

I can be myself with my partner and I am not judged.

Now these sentences are a lot better because you have detailed what you mean by the word 'nice' and made it more descriptive. Why is reasoning important? Every time you want something, do ask yourself questions like why, how, where, when, what? These questions are loaded with emotions.

Suppose, you want a house.

Ask yourself, where you want the house to be – country, state and location. Ask yourself, why you want it there.

Maybe, it's close to your workplace or your kids' school, or it's surrounded by nature or it houses the view of a waterfall, or it's closer to the beach or it's an upscale location where you have dreamt of living all your life. Ask yourself how many rooms you would like to have in the house. What décor do you want?

In the event that you want an adventurous guy, ask yourself why. It is because you love trying different things, you are crazy about experimenting different activities, or you are eager to live life with some thrill and just thinking about it lights up your face The feelings created even when you merely think like that, makes you realize that you got your answer. Ask questions and you will get the right answers. Reason with yourself.

Once you have lived the feelings associated with your desire, simply list your desirable thoughts, sit back and let Nature play its role. You are bound to love the outcome. Trust me on it.

20. THE DOS AND DON'TS

There are lots of people who do not know what they want in life but they are quick to point out what they do not want in their lives.

If the above sentence reminds you of yourself, write down the few things you want on one side of the sheet and write down the long list of what you don't want in your life on the other side. Keep writing until you have exhausted your list of *what you do not want* in your life because for some of you, that will spring up rather easily and effortlessly.

Once you have defined what you want and what you do not want in your life, it simplifies things and puts you in a more positive mind frame.

Firstly, you need to go point by point and change your 'do not want' into 'want.'

Consider these sample points from the perspective of attracting a partner:

Do not want – someone whose priority is work, work and more work.

What you need to change here is that you want someone who can balance his professional as well as his personal life.

Do not want – someone who is fat.

What you mean here is that you are looking for someone who is health conscious and fit.

Do not want – someone who is too quiet.

What you mean here is that you are looking for someone who is outgoing, communicative, interactive and fun to be with.

What you are doing here is changing the negatives to positives and gradually, there would not be any negative points left on your list. It is important to change the negatives to positives because you need to attract the right partner for you with these positive aspects rather than remain confused.

Secondly, the list must always highlight the *must-haves* without which you cannot do but one must also use common sense and consider it on a case-to-case basis.

For example, you are a dog lover, having two dogs at home.

In this case, you might want to attract a partner who likes dogs at all cost or else, there would be a clash of interest. In certain situations, you would need to make sure that the person you are attracting is someone who not only likes pets but they also like dogs for sure, or you might want to confirm that the person is not allergic to fur or animals in any way.

In the above instance, isn't it far better to compromise on the partner preference rather than the *must-haves*? In some cases, the must-haves cannot change. You would want it at all cost.

Thirdly, you can be extremely specific about the things you want as long as you know how to be flexible about your expectations. Weigh the possibilities before you rule him or her out because it is likely that he or she might be the one. You might not always get someone who matches your specification like a carbon copy but slight variations must be acceptable as per the need of the hour.

The point above brought an example to mind.

Meera was adamant about dating men with dark hair and light eyes and turned down a lot of men who didn't match it. Her best friend Shobha introduced her to her brother, Rahul.

Within a short time, Meera got along with Rahul like a house on fire and she began pursuing Rahul actively. They moved from the friend zone to exclusive dating.

The only glitch was that Rahul had light hair but their chemistry seemed to supersede the fact that he had blonde hair. Otherwise, he was a perfect match for her, including the light eyes.

The lack of dark hair didn't deter her from carrying forward with Rahul and they were so happy together. She deliberately chose to overlook her desire for dark-haired men although she was certain that Rahul would look much better with dark hair rather than the light hair he currently had.

One afternoon, Meera was invited to Rahul's house for lunch. She chanced upon a family picture and was surprised to see Rahul with dark hair. On complimenting about his hair color, she discovered that he had temporarily colored his hair light, a few times, for a change of style. He didn't have plans to keep it light anymore as he preferred his dark hair. This revelation and confession thrilled her.

So the message here is, don't overrule the fact that you might see reality with your eyes but it is likely to be far from reality.

Give the situation a fair chance. You never know what you get. What if Meera had to be adamant and refused the opportunity to acknowledge Rahul's chemistry with her only because he didn't fit one of her must-haves. She would have lost out on her chances of discovering her perfect guy.

Bend your rules. You need not stick to your list like glue. In specific cases, you need to change your outlook to suit the situation.

There are people with stiff specifications and do not budge from those. For instance, some of them insist on wanting a tattooed partner or someone with a piercing. My suggestion is that these are simple things and not big enough to reject someone outright, terming it to be a mismatch.

I know of a guy who is specifically looking for a girl who has her belly button pierced as it turns him on. Unfortunately, it is over five years and he is still searching! You are likely to miss out on some of them as you can hardly raise her top to check if her belly is pierced. Try not to be too adamant in what you want. People can change later and have their belly button pierced or a tattoo done for their partner. I know of people who do stuff they haven't done before, all because they have fallen madly in love. Temporary stuff can be incorporated with time.

Moreover, when you write what you want in your ideal partner, understand the reason why you need any particular trait in him or her. Do be flexible even if he or she might not have all the must-haves that you are looking for.

For example, you are a tea lover and despite asking for a partner who matches you to the 'T,' you will have to be open to minor changes like he could turn out to be a coffee drinker or it is likely that you drift off to sleep rather early and is an early riser, while he sleeps pretty late at night and wakes up the next day in time for lunch!

So be flexible with your list and also be open about adapting to any changes required whatsoever. I am giving you intrinsic details on how to go about it because there are lots of people who are struggling just to put their thoughts together and they need help in doing so. So here you are…

21. BELIEVE IN LOVE

You need to believe in love. The belief is essential as many of us are looking for an ideal partner, but deep down, you no longer believe in the concept of love. The reasons for this kind of a non-belief could be a failed love relationship in the past, or the experience of their parents and friends.

Whatever may be the belief, clear your mind of all negative thinking. If you have been rejected in relationships, you got to stop rejecting yourself. If the experiences of others stop you from discovering the most awesome feeling called love, you need to steer clear of mirroring such experiences as your own. You deserve the best. Therefore, give yourself a chance or give yourself several chances. Everyone is different. Everybody's experiences too are different.

You need to believe that you can have the dream relationship that is tailor-made only for you. You might not necessarily want to term him or her to be your soulmate but he or she is still your perfect partner. You need to believe that love exists and it also exists for you and for everyone else on planet Earth. You can't have or attract anything that you believe does not exist. Can you?

For instance, Rita has endured child abuse and practically disliked men, though deep down, she yearned for a loving relationship. On the insistence of her friends, she did make a list but wasn't convinced she is capable of attracting a kind man or a loving relationship. The thought process she harboured was obvious whenever she came across any instance of discussion where the man is at fault. She usually reacted so strongly and the hatred she had for them often stood out in her words, "I knew it. All men are the same. They are sick and want only one thing from women."

All men or all experiences are not the same. Many women have men around them like their dad or their brothers who are exemplary individuals. Don't they? Doesn't that go to show that good men do exist?

I hear a lot of people preparing a list, wanting a loving relationship, but speaking in contradiction to their desires every time they get a chance. Quit doing it if you are one of them. If something is really bothering you, get help. Resolve it, heal from it and then get back to being ready to welcome the perfect man or woman in your life.

It is never too late to change your innermost thoughts on love because after all, it is meant for each and every person.

Just believe you are made for great love. You are made to be loved by someone equally mind-blowing as yourself. The more you believe, the more possible it appears.

Some of you might have been hurt in the past and have closed your doors to love. You have concluded that love is not meant for you. There are many of us who have experienced hurt while in love but it's not the end. You need to evaluate and see past your wounds. You need to come into terms with what happened. Heal yourself and rebuild the desire to love or be loved in return.

The easiest way to begin your healing is to get counselling, help or notice and acknowledge the pattern that's reflected by you in relationships. Accept your fault if your behavior seems impractical to you from a relationship standpoint.

Analyze your partner's behavior too. Be fair and if you think the relationship could have worked out, then note down the areas that require improvement so that you gain clarity. You would need these facts as a reference point for your future relationships. Consider it a learning experience. It is a lesson that will allow you to experience a more fulfilling love life.

Accepting yourself is very important.

Write down how, when and where would the two of you go for your first date! Pen down your dream date with the outfit you plan to wear and the entire sequence of events, almost like a script!

Read the script, imagine it, feel it. If you are smiling after you are done, and some of you have goose bumps all over your body, rest assured you are doing fine.

Planning is important. You need to plan. How do you want to look on your dream date? What do you plan to wear on your dream date? If you are a woman, pick the attire, the hairdo, the shoes, the purse and perfume. Plan everything right up to the nail color. There is no scope for anything to go haywire. If you have everything that's needed for the date, then you can move to the next step, and that is planning.

Treat yourself the best and people around you are going to treat you the way you treat yourself. You have *to be the potential perfect partner* for the man or woman who comes into your life.

I have known people who buy the most stylish clothes, have expensive shoes and have a collection of the best things but keep everything on hold because they are looking forward to that special person to come into their life before they wear it. Quit doing that and enjoy your life even in the absence of a partner. The minute you are enjoying your life, the desired partner will appear magically on the scene.

If you want to attract a fantastic relationship, then you must feel and live your life fantastically even before your partner comes in. Your life is happening now, so refrain from putting your life on hold until the partner comes along.

Love is made for everyone and you are no different. Go for it. Go all out. Believe with your heart and it is yours. It is yours forever.

22. ACT ON YOUR DESIRE

You have asked for a partner and have made your final list. You have made it your priority to feel and look good every day. Now you are getting yourself all ready for the partner to appear. Good.

What kind of a person are you looking for? Are you looking for a fun-loving person? Are you a fun person yourself? If not, then first become one yourself.

Great expectations will just not suffice; you got to act upon it. If you want to date an amazing person, you got to be amazing yourself. If you want to attract a partner with a positive outlook about life, you got to have a similar approach to life first. If you are not what you are looking for, you need to put in an effort to become someone close to what you are looking for before you attempt to attract anyone in your life.

If you are filled with unhappy thoughts all through the day, it is unlikely you can attract a partner with a happy outlook towards life. You have to match the vibration or be in sync with whatever you are attempting to attract. At the same time, it's not about becoming what you are not; it's about getting rid of the conditions that prevent you from being the real beautiful person that you are. Everyone is created by the Divine Being. Therefore, everyone is a beautiful soul that is capable of being awesome. So act on your desires.

Similarly, if you are seeking to date someone who is employed in a multinational, then you need to show up where there is a likely possibility to meet the person who matches your requirement. Leave your location or country if needed and base yourself in the area where the chances of meeting corporate professionals are high. Join groups where such people flock to.

If you are searching for a partner, join clubs that match your taste, show up at stores, shopping malls, parties, and act on your desire because watching romantic soaps on television or being indoor 24/7 or not getting out of your comfort zone or home is unlikely to get you the person you want. Act on your desires and step out of your house. Be open to meeting people who are introduced to you through common friends. Go for blind dates. Do everything that it takes to find your special person. You won't find your partner if you choose to remain within the four walls of your house. Put in your side of the effort unfailingly.

For example, Radha, grew up in a remote village of

Kerala but liked everything that is North Indian. She loved North Indian food, language and culture and always harboured a secret interest to settle down with a North Indian man. She spent all her growing years studying in Kerala. After completing her studies, she worked as a nurse at a nearby hospital until one of her friends Mini who worked with her, decided to leave Kerala and move to a Delhi-based hospital in search of better prospects.

Radha, being very close friends with Mini, joined her a few months later. Today Radha is settled in Delhi (North India), happily married to a Punjabi and has two lovely kids. When Mini moved to Delhi and informed Radha that there were vacancies in the hospital that she had joined, Radha realised that if she wanted a partner who is North Indian or wished to settle in the North, she got to make a move and wasting no time, she acted upon it.

You possibly cannot continue staying in a village in Kerala and work in a nearby small town, where practically everyone around you is predominantly a Keralite, and expect to meet a North Indian. You could meet a North Indian, taking into account the infinite possibilities that the Universe offers.

However, as Radha failed to meet anyone until her professional life had begun, she knew she had to move to the North for easy access to manifest her desires. When there is a need to act, or if there is a nudge from the Universe, you must act upon it.

There you are, all good to go!

23. THE POWER OF WATER

Water is one of the natural resources that has the capability to manifest your desires. Water is known to have a memory. Water has consciousness. Using water to attract anything in your life is another powerful means to achieve your desires.

You can programme water and manifest your desires. 60% of our body is made up of water. Water reacts to anything and everything that it is stored in. Similarly, as our body is constituted predominantly of water, it absorbs our thoughts, be it negative or positive. So there is an undeniable connection between our thoughts and our body.

Many a time, if we are not getting what we want, it could be that our thoughts are not in sync with what we want to experience. You can use water to charge your body and get whatever results you seek. There was an experiment done by Dr. Masaru Emoto. He exposed music, words spoken and typed, and videos to water and after it was crystallised, the water's response was highly impressive. Every positive word like gratitude, love and happiness was far more symmetrical and aesthetically pleasing than anything negative like anger, hatred and others.

You can take a piece of paper and write anything that you want on

107

it. Do note that it has to be something positive. Then tape it on the bottle or glass or pot or the vessel where you store the water for you to drink. You can leave it for a few hours or overnight. Remember what you write on the paper is what you become or get. It does not matter if you freeze the water or leave it as it is. You can drink this water the next day.

Try to ensure that the water is stored in a glass bottle or a copper glass or vessel and not in any plastic container. Some of you can get the water energies by leaving the bottle in the sun for a couple of hours. You can chant any mantra or prayer or speak to the water also before you consume it, in case you haven't pasted it on the glass. Leave the paper taped on the glass and fill fresh water in it for your next use. Keep doing this until what you want is achieved. Only ensure that the water is absolutely clean as you would be drinking the water.

You can consciously charge your water with gratitude or happy thoughts or your aspirations as water can be charged. The more you infuse yourself with gratitude, the more you are likely to attract that in your life. By doing this, you are aligning yourself to your expectations.

You have to believe that your good intent is going into the water and when you drink it, it is going to remain in your body, and so that's the vibration that you would want to resonate. If you put in gratitude for what you already have, you will receive more reasons to be grateful wherein your expectations and desires will be eventually fulfilled as well.

Besides that, you can also put your intention in another way. What you need here is a glass of water, pen and a piece of paper. Write your intention on the paper with a realistic date by which you want it to be manifested. If it's a job you are seeking, you can write "I want a job at XYZ organisation by date/month/year" on the paper and put the pen aside.

Place both your palms, facing each other, and rub them against each other, and all along chant mentally or aloud what you want or desire that you have written on the paper. Continue rubbing your hands together until your hands turn warm and you can't rub them against each other anymore. Your hand is energised. Now you must transfer the energy to the water in the glass.

You can do it in two ways. Firstly, place the paper on the floor and place the glass on the paper. Make sure that the bottom of the glass is not wet and wrap both your hands around the glass or you could alternatively wrap the paper around the glass of water and keep it in place with both your hands. Your hands are energised and the energy moves on to the water along with the words you have written.

Keep your hands around the glass of water and either affirm or visualise what you want for the next couple of minutes. Then drink the water.

You need to make sure only you drink the water, especially if you have asked for something specific. You can keep the paper aside for future use and you can do this as many times as you want to. Once the wish is fulfilled, bin the paper.

It will be of great help and your manifestation process will be easily simplified.

The power of water over our body is intense, powerful and miraculous. So go for it!

24. QUANTUM JUMPING

Quantum Jumping, discovered by Burt Goldman, is also called the two-cup method. Quantum jumping is the same as the manifestation method. It works with vibration, energy, frequency and rhythm just like the manifestation process. You are always broadcasting a signal. You are broadcasting a signal of unhappiness, sorrow, stress, failure and jealousy that are termed negative in nature. On the other hand, you are giving out a signal of happiness, peace, success, satisfaction, fulfilment and many others which are positive in nature.

Quantum jumping and manifestation are one and the same thing, and works on the same principle. Quantum Jumping is tuning yourself from your current situation of life to the situation you desire to be. Quantum jumping is moving across several parallel Universes and manifesting your reality.

You can do this experiment which has proved fruitful for several people.

Take two empty cups. One stands for the current situation in your life and the other cup is the anticipated situation of your life.

Cup A – stands for (current state) "I have a current job that sucks."

Cup B – stands for (desired state) "I desire my dream job at XYZ."

Paste the labels on the respective cups. You can read it out aloud or mentally. Fill water in cup A. Hold the glass and speak about your current job and your unhappy state about it. "I have a current job that sucks and I am not happy at all." The water can be any level but it has to be drinking water. Time is not a constraint. Therefore, say aloud in your mind as many statements as you wish.

Then take the water that is in cup A and pour it into cup B, the cup stands to bring forth your anticipated future or wish. Declare what you wrote on the cup aloud. "I desire a job with XYZ as soon as possible where I am extremely happy." Say it a couple of times as if you are affirming it or you could add more sentences to it. Then drink the water from Cup B. Some people pour water in both the cups and empty the water from Cup A into the desired cup or cup B which already has water and drink the whole thing. There are others who pour a few drops in their bath too from the desired cup B before they drink the remaining left in Cup B. Anyway, it works.

Most importantly, you need to act on it no matter what. Like in the case of the above example, you need to apply to the place or for the dream job after you do this exercise. Or you could even apply before you drink this. It doesn't matter. You can do it any number of times. You change the negative current situation to a positive futuristic situation. The combination of feeling, belief and intention is what matters here.

Water has the ability to energise you. So go for it. You can attract everything you wish for because this beautiful life is miraculous, abundant and worthy of living! Live it to your fullest, filled with happiness, joy and endless laughter. You are the creator of your life. Use your magic wand and make your life truly magnificent!

BOOKS BY THIS AUTHOR

A Few Hours Of Smart Work Or A Lifetime Of Hard Work?

https://www.amazon.com/dp/B084HLL8KS

Love Without Warning: A Collection Of Short Stories

https://www.amazon.com/dp/B084MLHBMD